CONTINUE

CONTINUE

GRAHAM FULTON

Published by Penniless Press Publications 2015

© Graham Fulton 2015

The author asserts his moral right to be identified as the author of the work.

All rights reserved. No part of this publication may be reproduced, stored in a retrieval system or transmitted in any form or by any means, electronic, mechanical, photocopying, recording or otherwise, without the prior permission of the publishers

ISBN 978-1- 326-18276-2

Cover photo: Bread – Graham Fulton
Back cover author photo by Helen Nathaniel-Fulton

Some of these poems have been published before
in *The Echo Room, Earth Love, Gutter* and the pamphlets
Speed of Dark (Controlled Explosion Press, 2012)
The Universe is a Silly Place (Controlled Explosion Press, 2013)

for

Tracy Patrick

and

Mandy Sykes

CONTENTS

Einstein's Daughter	11
The Man on the Other Side	12
Shit Happens	13
Pixellated	14
I Couldn't Write Anything Like This in a Zillion Years	16
A Bit Twitchy	18
National Poetry Day	19
The Story of Mulder and Scully Without Having to Watch the Entire Nine Seasons	20
A Film	23
Rain Dance	24
Diamond	25
From the Pavement	26
The Olympic Torch isn't Coming Through Paisley	27
At Home With the Morlocks	29
Good and Evil on the 7 McGill's	30
Flying	31
One Girl Platoon	32
The Boxer	33
Dog Botherer	34
Pagan	35
The Moon on My Shoe	36
55 Years a Wanker	38
Local Undead	40
Trying to Think of a Name	42
Gun Culture	43
Raging Bullshit	44
The Proust Casuals	46
Some Popular Countryside Sayings That Have Been Airbrushed from History	47
Daleks at the *Free From* Section of *Tesco*	48
Devil Dogs Hooked on Heroin!	50
The Paisley Address	52
Incubator	54
Drips	56

Mary McNair	57
High Energy	58
A Gent in Ned's Clothing	59
Someone in *Iceland* is Stinking of Shit	60
Four Avocados of the Apocalypse	62
The Story of Religion Without Having to Believe in Anything	64
Everywhere	69
Unreality Check	70
Resurrection Men	72
Self Explanatory	74
Tour de Paisley	76
At the Third Stroke	77
Requiem for the Fallen	78
Wealth of Nations	80
The Knowledge	81
The Edge	82
Divided Selfie	83
Social Comment	84
Catholic Pigeon	85
George Square Thatcher Death Horse	86
Mogwai CDs Covered in Dust	87
Fine	88
The Story of Human Afflictions Without Having to Catch Any of Them	90
Club Arthritis	93
Welcome to Pointless	95
Withdrawal Symptom	97
The Bank	98
Large Hardon Collider	100
Suddenly I Remember The Dog and The Man	102
Complete Dummy	104
Tenements of Mars	105
Micro Biology	106

Einstein's Daughter

a wee blonde girl
walking out with
her dad

working out life
in her logical
head

2 times nothing is nothing
2 times 1 is 2
2 times 2 is 4
2 times 3 is 6
2 times 5 is 8

2 times 5   is 8

2 times   5   is   8

2 times   5   is

2 times nothing is nothing

The Man on the Other Side

the pavement   the man
the phlegm

landing on
the pavement   the sound

Shit Happens

a woman with
her back to me

wearing a red cagoule
with the hood up

is wiping something
white and large

from the window
of her lounge

with a
yellow cloth

Pixellated

I've been rejected, informed
I'm totally unacceptable,
there aren't enough pixels
in my face, my face
is not thereany more, it's
folding in
on
itself,
there aren't enough pixels
in the day,
nothing to get a hold of,
itisn'rtt good enough
I am

out in the rain
wealiking down long strange pavements
past
schoolkids hustling for cigarettes
benrt and broken umbrellas
a telephone box with no door
to find someone kind who can
fill me withn pixels
make me wjole,
acceptable unrejected,
fit
in,   no more
an outsider with not enough
pixels

are
the way to heaven,
contentment acceptance,
my life is disintig grating
I hasve to find mrte pixels i
have tpo finde

someone to give me more pixels,
give me the thing
I'm sadly lacking
pixels,
beautiful pixxills,
dots of illusion,
solid light,
Ihave the right ot be acceptable

I Couldn't Write Anything Like This in a Zillion Years

the Estonian postman comes to the door.
the poetry quarterly
thumps on
the floor,
and I tear it open
and turn the pages in a frenzy
and look at the poems and think
that I can never write stuff as good
as that in a zillion years
and why can't I write poems like that
and why is my stuff a load of shite
and turn more and more pristine pages
and read more and more pristine poems
about fascinating impenetrable subjects
by people
from Swindon and England
who have recently been published by
household name publishing empires
at the drop of a hat.
and see how metrically structured
they all are
and how intellectually conceived
in form and language with Capital Letters
at the start of each line they all are
and how I can only scratch
a load of pish
a hamster could write.
and why
can't I create stiff-upper-lip verses
that look all University Challenge and Jeremy-
Paxman-your-starter-for-ten and cute-teddy-bear-
mascot-wearing-a-scarf and academic
on the subtly graded slightly off-white paper
and why
did my granny die

and why is there no peace in the world
and why can't I stop using the word and
and why can't I stop using swear words
and why can't I stop using fucking swear words.
and why
can't I write the bestselling biography
of a dead Poet Laureate
or a National Bard
and why can't I do *Waste Land*-length poems
about the mysterious process of writing poems
which is the last resort of the successfully-desperate,
and I've just put an illogical comma
in the correct place,
and I've just gone back to the start and changed
a million years into *a zillion years*
and *thumps on my floor* into *thumps on the floor*
for some reason that completely escapes me.
and why can't I ever make poems
all measured and proper and meant-to-be-this-
way and finish
this fucking pile of crap where it's meant
to finish.

A Bit Twitchy

the printer has jammed the modern world has jammed
and I'm trying to print this poem out
but the printer has jammed
and I've got to reset the paper
in the tray
and it's going to jam again,
I know it's going to jam
again.
and I've developed a twitch
on the lower lid
of my left eye
I can
feel it twitching,
I can
see it twit-
ching,
I know it's going
to keep on twitching for as long as
the printer keeps jamming
and the paper is all crunched up
and out of alignment
and the paper is almost gone
and a box at the lower right corner of the screen
is eagerly informing me
the ink is at an end-of-the-world-
as-we-know-it
level.
and I can feel my left eyelid twitching,
and it's going to keep on twitching
because the printer is jammed
and there's nobody here
to help me
please help me
and my eyelid is twitching
my left eyelid is twitching I can feel my eyelid twitching.

National Poetry Day

On national poetry day
I went to *Morrisons* and bought
Two tins of baked beans
Two tins of mushy peas,
Three tins of lean corned beef
With a ring pull on each,
One pack of lean minced steak
One pack of liver
One pack of ten slices
of non-vegetarian bacon,
Living coriander,
Two dead haddock fillets
Two dead salmon fillets,
Three peppers in hallucinogenic colours
One medium sized cauliflower I had to search for
For ages
But was determined to find myself
Without asking,
One loaf of designer bread,
Twelve large caged hen eggs
Which I checked to see if any were cracked
And a 4-pack of non-recyclable toilet rolls
For when I shit it all out again,
Then chatted poetically about the weather
With the taxi driver who carried me home
Where I remembered I'd forgotten
All about the bloody tartare sauce
But I'm buggered if I'm going back

**The Story of Mulder and Scully Without
Having to Watch the Entire Nine Seasons**

you got your clones
you got your hybrids
you got your rebels

you got your shapeshifters
you got your bounty hunters
you got your abductees

you got your vicious baby aliens
you got your old unhappy aliens
you got your aliens trapped in the ice

you got your doggett
you got your krycek
you got your skinman

you got your lone gunmen
you got your super soldiers
you got your baby messiah

you got your black oil
you got your green gas
you got your killer bees

you got your smallpox
you got your vaccine
you got your implants

you got your bodies in tanks
you got your navajos
you got your crucifix

you got your colonisation
you got your syndicate
you got your shadow government

you got your virus
you got your tunguska
you got your roswell

you got your smoking man
you got your well-dressed man
you got your deep throat

you got your spike in the neck
you got your mulder's dad
you got your mulder's real dad

you got your long black coats
you got your platform shoes
you got your weird experiments

you got your foetuses in jars
you got your cancer
you got your genetic mutations

you got your missing nine minutes
you got your missing sister
you got your gibster

you got your autopsies
you got your veronica cartwright
you got your martin landau

you got your half man half worm
you got your slug on the spine
you got your man who can
squeeze through drainpipes

you got your human replacements
you got your sunflower seeds
you got your 'I Made This!'

you got your queequeg
you got your starbuck
you got your desperately-looking-for-something-you-can-never-find-moby-dick-type-references

you got your minor-characters-who-say-frickin-instead-of-fuckin
you got your so-bloody-dark-most-of-the-time-it's-impossible-to-make-anything-out
you got your sitting-with-the-curtains-closed-for-the-rest-of-your-life-as-you-try-to-discover-what-the-frick-is-going-on

you got your will-they-won't-they-have-a-shag
you got your movie-spin-off-between-seasons-5-and-6
you got your gagging-for-a-glimpse-of-gillian-anderson's-under-wear

you got your out there

you got your truth

you got your nice wee tune

(whistle the X-Files theme tune)

A Film
Text message from Helen

amazing thing in
              the cab a very
                            catchy beat of a
song playing and I
saw a woman
              walking 2 long
                            haired dogs and
they were
shoogling along
              hair swinging to
                            the beat then a
smart woman
tottering along on
              too high heels to
                            the beat and then a
young sporty girl
then a dwarf on
              crutches if only I
                            could have made a
film

Rain Dance

A double rainbow,
high sullen clouds.

Show off seagulls,
silver with wings,

thump on the roof
of our low rise flat.

Diamond

8 in the morning

a woman in her

fifties or
sixties

mental or
drunk

going up Greenlaw
singing

*I'd much
rather be*

*forever in
blue jeans*

From the Pavement

I pick a pair
of pink footprints –

        cardboard perfume

a cartoon freshener
chucked from a car

the scent of memory
sticks to my fingers –

        distant detachment

somebody else's
adult and child

chewable strawberry
factory fruits –

        an undersmell

the reek of
ingrown cigarettes

nicotine nostalgia

The Olympic Torch isn't Coming Through Paisley

Lord Coe and Co. have pronounced
with their big smiling Conservative teeth
that the Olympic Torch isn't coming through Paisley
in case the torch bearer
with his athletic shorts and healthy grin
is confronted
by a tsunami of zombies
disguised as neds   junkies   jakies
beggars   buskers   big issue salesmen
staggering men
single mothers pushing prams
forgotten pensioners pushing walkers
in unstoppable numbers
out of the shadows and closes
and gap sites
shops
that have been empty for years
and the overflowing job centre
of a once-proud town
making a hideous keening sound
with arms outstretched
and palms upturned
looking for benefits
burgers
medicine
methadone
work   hope
and tearing the golden beacon
of privilege from his grasp
and pissing on it until it sizzles out
because we must only show
the shortbread tin illusion
and the shaggy highland cows
and people dancing in kilts
and nice monsters and snow capped mountains

and must never suggest
that all is not all right in the dark heart of Britain
because the world loves Britain
and has always loved Britain
and anything that damages that undying love
for everything that is Great about Britain
must be hidden away

At Home With The Morlocks

the tumble drier is full of things
tumbling
in the corner of the kitchen
at nine in the morning,
and it's making
a far off throbbing
heart beat sound
as it tumbles
and tumbles
and dries
and dries
which also
reminds me
of the Morlock machinery
from *The Time Machine*
that Rod Taylor could hear
as he climbed down a hole
to try and rescue Weena
from a fate worse than death,
and I can see
the poor old Morlocks
standing there in their dismal
post-obliteration underground chamber
and opening up their tumble driers
and pressing the soft fluffy towels
and frilly underwear with a fragrance
of spring meadows
and cool running mountain streams
against their yearning blue mutated faces
before preparing a tasty
Eloi coq au vin and cheesecake
and thinking it doesn't get
any better than this at
the precise moment Rod Taylor
runs in and sets them on fire

Good and Evil on the 7 McGill's

a girl
    wearing
   a hooded top
with cartoons
      of Spider-Man,
   Iron Man,
and the timeless messages
            THWACK!
      WHAAAM!
READY FOR ACTION!
  splashed
all over
it
 is reading
  a Penguin Classics
            Dracula
      and listening to
    her iphone
at the same time

Flying

a young daytime drunk
at the back of the bus is singing
Life's a piece uv shit
                but ah kin deal wi it
to a not-quite-as-drunk young daytime drunk
at the back of the bus
who says in retaliation
It's no
Life's a piece uv shit
                but ah kin deal wi it –
it's
Life's a piece uv shit
                when yi look at it –
                fur fuck's sake
git it right!

but he goes on singing it
the wrong way anyway

One Girl Platoon

a hoodie who looks like
Willem Dafoe

reading a METRO
and picking her nose

The Boxer

a mist it
a mist ma bus beekawzuv HIM
AYE   HIM THERE

its aw hiz fault

look at thay eyes
he knows am talkin aboot im
an aw that pishin eez bin dayn

av nevur seen anythin like it
aw that pishin on thi pavement
thurz nay need fur it
at this time in thi mornin

it jist goes on an on

thi vet huzni a clue

                    LOOK
he knows wur talkin aboot im

am goin ti git ma hair done
an eez made me miss ma bus
wi aw that pishin eez bin dayn
on thi pavement

am no bein cruel
its jist thi way he iz
wi aw that pishin

its no real   aw that pishin
its no real

Dog Botherer

the dog at a window
                barking at daylight

barking, I believe,
           at me
for being out here,
         alive,
            its
eyes following mine,
my eyes following
              its,
        the head
infinitesimally moving
in the direction
I'm walking until I'm absent
from sight
          then
                  silence

I'll circle around
          and do this again,
just to make sure
        it knows it's me,
              just
        to
    rub it
in

Pagan

my *Twix* wrapper
                is swooshed from my grip, flies
ridiculously fast across the grass, whips
impressively fast over
the edge
of the hill where Howwood Temple
has existed
        since 1760 –
                a stone folly, or shrine,
where I'm trying to swallow my lunch
as the fag-end of Hurricane Bertha
spanks me about
and two German cyclists tight in Lycra
are skipping around
whistling, smiling, obviously hoping
to have a frantic fuck in the mud,
some ancient hanky-panky
once I'm gone, it's what
we're good at, it's what
                we're here for,
to procreate inside an old ruin
with eight sides, delightful arch windows,
obligatory empty can of cider
and a pink sprayed-on ban-the-bomb symbol –
                          peace and love,
fuck that, they can hope all they want,
I'm going nowhere!

The Moon on My Shoe

There's a cold
divinely circular circle
of chemical paste
on my right shoe,
                     the same one
I have trouble
tying the shoelaces of –
                          it must
          have fallen
like an angel
from my teeth
when I was brushing my mouth
this morning
and has dwelt there
                           ever since –
         I don't think
anyone else
will have noticed
as I haven't been
out of the house today
                    and if you
     screw up
your eyes
and make the world
around the shoe
          a blur,
          ignore
the information
logic is feeding you
then it looks just like
a moon hanging in a Paisley sky
or a body such as Venus
                         or even
              one of
the ones they've

only given a number to —
                    the lace eyes
                 could
     be black holes —
yes —
the laces could be worm holes
you can catch a bus through
to a better universe
with no war or hunger
or deity-based religions —
                         or sexually
                transmitted
      diseases,
or shoes

55 Years a Wanker

It's true!
      I've proved it!
            You can
be born and reach
         the age of 55
and be a total wanker
            for all the time in between
It's true!
      I've proved it!
You can
      arse about forever
with a big smile on your face
You can
      go bouncing happily
towards oblivion
You can
      search day after day
for the perfect smoked ham
            and mustard sandwich
in *Tesco*
      with just the right consistency
of mustard
You can
      sit on the pan
and not realise there's no toilet paper
            until you've finished
You can
      spend your afternoons
watching episodes of *The Walking Dead*
You can
      blubber every time
at the end of *Field of Dreams*
You can
      push through the noise
and see everything clearly

                        You can
            write the word
wanker
wanker wanker wanker wanker
winker wanker wunker
wanker   wanker   woonker
wank   wink   wank   wink
until it turns into a sort of
Edwin Morgany-type concrete poem
only not as good
It's true!
            I've proved it!

Local Undead
Text Messages from Helen as She Goes to Work

Loony attacking
phone boxes
outside Gilmour
Street

Excellent

Junkie getting
some coins

He has enough for
a bag I think so
he's gone now

*

Man on bus looks
like nosferatu
guzzling a pie

surreal

And just saw
ambulance taking
away what looked
like a dead lady

from paisley
centre

*

V v unattractive
man on bus with a

this is my pulling t
shirt on

Oh dear
Pulling his plonker
it must be

*

You can't see
the two prams and
the elderly man's
pusher or hear

the kids crying

he's stopping now
to take on more
it's uncannily
like Kenya 30

years ago
and people can't
now get off

Trying to Think of a Name

for a poem
about the busker I've just passed
who's courageously chopping away
at his five string acoustic
while singing
Baby Now That I've Found You
by The Foundations

but all
I can think of
is *Songs in the Key of Shite*

Gun Culture

a tiny shiny
silver
pistol

with
a plastic indian's
head on
the handle

lies
broken
on
the
    shopping
        centre steps

Raging Bullshit

a red car stops in
the middle of
the road and
a man gets in at
the passenger side
at the same time
a blue car pulls
up behind it and
honks its horn
and the red car
moves off and
indicates and
turns right and
comes to a halt
and the blue car
moves off and
indicates and
turns right and
comes to a halt
alongside
the red car
and the driver
of the red car
brings down
his window
and sticks his
arm out and
makes a *You're
a total
wanker* gesture
with his arm going
up and down and
the blue car drives
away and the red
car drives away

and they'll never
see each other
ever again

The Proust Casuals

two seconds
after Helen says
*Maybe it's a meeting of
the Proust Appreciation Society*

four paralytic
football supporters
start chanting *PROUST! PROUST!*
on the six o'clock train to Paisley

**Some Popular Countryside Sayings
That Have Been Airbrushed from History**

If the geese fly south in the Autumn sky
ye must eat some pumpkin pie
If the rain doth pour and the wind doth fart
tie your donkey to a cart

If the clouds in the western sky are white
go and do a massive shite
If there's just one cornflake left in the box
go and slaughter a helpless fox

If the fairies dance in the dingly glade
smash a badger's head with a spade
If the frost doth come and the wind doth trumpet
pour some petrol over a strumpet

If the ducks do waddle in single file
go and string up a paedophile
If the west wind blow and your nose doth twitch
go and burn an innocent witch

If the sun in the eastern sky be red
take your sister to your bed
If the sky be blue and the north wind peeps
go and have oral sex with a sheep

If the new born lambs doth leap and frolic
go and become an alcoholic
If the bees from yonder meadow doth flee
go on a random killing spree

If the sky be full of darkness and death
go and take some crystal meth
If the sun doth rise beyond the hills
end it all with a bucket of pills

Daleks at the *Free From* Section of *Tesco*

To be spoken in two separate voices.
One to be deep and menacing.
One to be shrill and hysterical.

We must find some Gluten Free

    We must find some Gluten Free!

We must find some of
Mrs. Crimble's Gluten Free Crackers
which are perfect along with
Welsh Mature Cheese-free Cheese

    They do not have any!

They do not have any!

    They do not have any!

What the fuck do you mean
they do not have any!

    We must exterminate the nearest
    Gluten Free assistant!

I have a sensitive tummy
This means we will have to make do
with Gluten Free Cheese Oatcakes
because I don't like
the Herb and Seed Oatcakes
They give me the boak

    They give him the boak!

They give me the boak

They give him the boak!

Do they have any
yummy Gluten Free Peanut Butter?

There is no such thing as Gluten Free Peanut Butter!

Yes there is
it's right next to
the Gluten Free Spam
and the Gluten Free Pot Noodle
and the Gluten Free Cup A Soup
and the Gluten Free Horse Burgers
and the Gluten Free Washing Up Liquid
and the Gluten Free Feminine Wipes
and the Gluten Free Gluten

We must eradicate all Gluten from the Universe!

If there's one thing I can't tolerate
it's the Gluten Free Rice Cakes
They taste of cardboard
and they give me diarrhoea!

Diarrhoea!

Diarrhoea

Diarrhoea!

They give me diarrhoea
and they have to be exterminated

Exterminate the Rice Cakes!

Exterminate the Rice Cakes!

Exterminate! Masticate! *Regurgitate!* Defecate!

Devil Dogs Hooked on Heroin!

is the headline in today's paper
(except for the exclamation mark)
which makes me think
of West Highland Terriers
and Chihuahuas
lying around
on their backs
in dark flats
surrounded by drug baggage
such as needles and spoons
and wondering what the stuff is going on
with dead eyes
and sappy smiles
and no need to take any further part
in the lovely fabric of society.
or going
to Yorkie coke snorting clubs
or queuing up at high street chemists
or checking themselves
into trendy rehab
teacup puppy accessory clinics
along with brain mush rock stars
and not funny comedians
and total fat cat bankers.
and the words
inside
go on to say that
dealers give the dogs the drug
for a laugh to see what happens
or to make them more aggressive
so they eventually become insane
and have to be put down and
there's a picture of a Staffie
with its nose pressed against
the mesh of the cage staring

straight into the camera and wondering
just how low humans can go.

The Paisley Address

went ti see *Lincoln* last night
an a huv ti say
thi Big Danster wuz fuckin magic
he got im
spot on
with iz sad eyes like thi wanz
in thi photies by Alexander Gardner
who came fay Paisley
by thi way
an iz acksent wuz fuckin eckselunt
a mickschur uv
Kentucky an Illinois
an thi bit wi thi thurteenth amendmunt
whin they finally abolish slavery
furevur
brought a fuckin tear ti ma eye
az did thi bit
fay thi Gehteezburg Address
whinny goes on aboot
guvurnmunt uv thi peepil by thi peepil
fur thi peepil
a think
thur shud deffinetley be even mair films
aboot thi embreeonick unitit states
they cud day a whole seereez
includin wan aboot
thi emancipayshun proclamayshun
ur thi reconstruckshun
ur thi inspurayshunnul abolishun speeches
uv Frederick Douglass
also known az *The Fredlar* by iz pals
GAUN YURSEL BIG MAN!
am goin ti see it
again ramorra
me an ma mates huv hired a speshul mini bus

wir gonni take a cayrioot
an git totally fuckin steamboats ya dancer!

Incubator

the grandfather and
           his granddaughter
on a nice day out
             walk the length
      of the bendy bus
and sit
   on the seat
opposite
       a girl with scraped-
back ginger hair
         who's communicating loudly
into her phone
      and saying
heez gonni git a fuckin batterin
                    am tellin yi
         heez gonni git a fuckin batterin
                heez gonni git a fuckin batterin
    am tellin yi

the granddaughter and
             her grandfather
quietly stand
      and walk back down
the length of the bus
          and sit on the seat
opposite a man
     with an incubator
    for reptile eggs
and possibly
      a bag of termites on his knee,
I can't make out
      the label
at this distance,
      while outside the window
a black Labrador

                    is taking a dump
on the grass

Drips

I'm at the counter to get
                my LOTTERY ticket
and NOKIA Top Up
                and WATER is coming
through the TESCO roof
                and landing on
my head,
    shoulders,
and running down
                the back of my NECK
and I tell the assistant
                who looks at me as if
I'm mentally defective
                or emotionally immature,
and it occurs
to me
   that this could be
a convenient METAPHOR
                for the way we let
the seconds,
      years, of our lives
splatter away,
        and I'll write a POEM about it
when I get home,
            but when I got home
I couldn't be arsed

Mary McNair

the old lady says to herself
For Goodness Sake
                Mary McNair

half a moment
after tripping over
               her feet
as she opens the door
to Marks and Spencer

at ease
with the consistency of her life
for catching
her unawares

High Energy

as he skips between
the floor mops
bin numbers
low
energy bulbs

a knee-high boy shouts
COME OAN COME OAN
AM NO TELLIN YI AGAIN

followed by
COME OAN COME OAN
AM NO TELLIN YI AGAIN

to his pissed-off mum
two light years behind

A Gent in Ned's Clothing

at 10.01 a.m.

a man

not a young man

in tracksuit bottoms
and tracksuit top

holds the door
of the Paisley Centre open
for two ladies

not young ladies

as he bellows
*WHIT FUCKIN TIME
DI YI CALL THIS!*

into his phone

Someone in *Iceland* is Stinking of Shit

I've got a longing for a potato scone.
A passing need
that will be gone
next week.

So in I go

but as I prowl the wonderful shelves
I detect
a distinct whiff of shit.
Mature shit.
Young shit.
All ages of shit.

Too much information
this early in the morning.

Safely
out of range
I look back and eye the suspects.

A respectable old lady
selecting her bacon
or an obvious man
of unguessable years.

It has to be him.
My stinker of choice.
That's his brand
if he's earned it
or not.

He's standing staring
at the margarines,
swaying slightly,

imagining what he can spread
on his potato scones
to make them
even more yummy
than they possibly are.

A kindred spirit.
A man of taste.

There are worse things to be.
Maybe it's me.

Four Avocados of the Apocalypse

on the way back
                        and
                                  I've got
four avocados in my bag
as I'm waiting on the pavement
with a young frantic man
looking left and right and left again
in the way he was taught
in his distant childhood
on the pavement
opposite
                                  who
gives me the distinct impression
he's on something serious
such as hard drugs
lucozade
or too much fried bread
as he stands there with
wild bug eyes   mad neck jerking,
he's suddenly
                still
                        and staring at me
with my British Red Cross bag
with the words
Unconditional care in a crisis
printed on it in white
and the four ready-to-eat avocados inside
which I know he's going to take
to create his own private guacamole
if I start to navigate the space
towards him
as he pulls out a machete in my head
and I know
                 I should turn
                        and run

but I start to cross instead

The Story of Religion Without Having to Believe in Anything

you got your adam
you got your eve
you got your fig leaf covering the genitals

you got your land of nod
you got your pillar of salt
you got your burning bush

you got your holy war
you got your holy smoke
you got your holy cow

you got your endless slaughter
you got your christians who hate muslims
you got your muslims who hate christians

you got your muslims who hate jews
you got your jews who hate muslims
you got your christians who hate jews

you got your hindus who hate muslims
you got your muslims who hate hindus
you got your nuclear capability

you got your ZOO
you got your NUTS
you got your OK!

you got your scientologists
you got your tom cruise
you got your john travolta

you got your gurus and lamas
you got your shakers and quakers
you got your fakirs and fakers

you got your christmas radio times
you got your writhing nuns
you got your climb every mountain

you got your charlton heston with a false beard
you got your max von sydow
you got your robert powell

you got your torture chambers
you got your spanish inquisition
you got your monty python's flying circus

you got your eye for an eye
you got your tooth for a tooth
you got your turn the other cheek

you got your jim jones
you got your kool-aid laced with cyanide
you got your father ted

you got your satanism
you got your shamanism
you got your ism after ism after ism

you got your moonies
you got your mormons
you got your shag anything that moves

you got your exorcist
you got your max von sydow again
you got your green projectile vomit

you got your seventh-day adventists
you got your sacred spaceship
you got your common-or-garden mass suicide

you got your wicker man
you got your waco
you got your martyrs fried alive

you got your jehovah's witness at the front door
you got your gideon's bible in the hotel drawer
you got your dancing about on glastonbury tor

you got your snakeoil evangelist
you got your tables of money
you got your all major credit cards accepted

you got your mahatma gandhi
you got your martin luther king
you got your people who mean what they believe

you got your orthodox
you got your unorthodox
you got your soap box

you got your karma
you got your nirvana
you got your kurt cobain

you got your do unto others
you got your paedophile bishops
you got your love thy neighbour

you got your jedi
you got your light sabre
you got your alec guinness saying
feel the force young skywalker

you got your omen
you got your damien - the omen II
you got your final conflict

you got your pilgrims trampled to death
you got your fatwā
you got your beheadings on youtube

you got your church of england
you got your church of scotland
you got your church of outer mongolia

you got your crusaders slicing up women and children
you got your extermination of indigenous peoples
you got your thou shalt not kill

you got your middle east peace process
you got your middle east peace process breaking down
you got your retaliatory strikes

you got your nice ideas disfigured
you got your handy excuse for male domination
you got your control through fear

you got your purgatory
you got your angels and demons
you got your eternal damnation for those whose face
doesn't fit

you got your red slippers covered in rubies
you got your wizard of oz
you got your flying monkeys

you-got-your-pope-who-colluded-with-the-nazis
you-got-your-wee-polish-pope-who-came-to-
glasgow-in-his-mobile-home
you-got-your-loads-of-other-popes-I-can't-
remember-the-names-of

you-got-your-orange-walk-and-tribal-drums
you-got-your-brainless-chants
you-got-your-why-don't-you-stay-at-home-and-read

a-good-book-instead

you got your gates of pearl
you got your pillars of wisdom

you-got-your-in-need-of-something-to-make-sense-
of-what-cannot-be-made-sense-of-in-order-to-
convince-yourself-you-can-survive-life

you got your let there be light
you got your original sin
you got your let there be shite

you got your god

you got your allah

you got your Big Enchilada of choice

Everywhere

I've heard the song *Everywhere*
by Fleetwood Mac
twice today,
the first being as I stared into
my STANDARD CAPPUCCINO
in *Sainsbury's*
the second being as I walked to buy
some GORDON'S GIN at *Tesco*
which is quite amazing
as it was
first released in 1987
and nobody in their right mind
should be listening to
their sublimely wrinkly soft rock
at this time in the morning.
it makes me think
that maybe
it's an important message
letting me know there's nothing
to be afraid of
and the universe is made up of
a massive shared spiritual consciousness
and everything is part of everything else,
or maybe
it's just Christine McVie
sensually inducing me
to go and buy a ticket
for their concert in Glasgow later this year
but someone I can't remember
told me that one ticket costs
about one hundred and fifty quid
so there's no way I'm doing that.

Unreality Check

It's very skull-bulging to think that when
I'm conclusively declared a dead body
some people I know
will still be existing in this
weird corporeal world moving
about their big business and
biting pies at half-
empty stadium football matches and
smiling and shagging each other's hot
and eager flesh and
acquiring daily newspapers
and factory production line crisps
and throwing sticks for
their bounding crossbreed dogs
in local dried-up water fountain parks
and not
giving
liberatingly unacademic free verse
a second thought because
they're full throttle alive
thrusting hopefully into tomorrow on trams and skateboards
and hovercrafts in their bone shells with fat throbbing brains
while I'm dead
it's strangely delightful
to accept that
I'll be off in dark timeless
spaceless nothingness wondering
where it is I am and going
Ooooh, where am I?, or not even
wondering because
I'll be dispensed with all over the cosmic shop
and won't be thinking and won't
be reunited with my dead relatives or even know
about smiling and touching and licking each other's
hot and lovely flesh because mine will be cold and ugly

or turned to soft white ash
and I won't remember that I ever
used to think or was ever even sitting here in the first place

Resurrection Men

Someone has something serious,
                              a rage,
against the idea of death,
                    of dying,
              has taken
    great exception,
has penetrated
a stone
or a
pole
into the big display window
of the Kelburne Funeral Home
with its
soothing, inevitable lettering,
certificates of authentication
and contented, peaceful
                        undertakers
happy to guide you,
                  over,
         to another
shore

                    Four
                 workers
with sparking tools,
short yellow ladders
and red and white cones
and humphing
a square slice of replacement glass
across the starred shards
are so entwined
with the delight of life,
                       of living,
             have taken
      no notice,

                        are not
the least bit sexually diverted,
                                aroused
                        by the idea
of the young
        blonde woman
                jogging past
in these rain-grey skin-shaped leggings,
rhythmic bottom,
swishing pony tail
as she glances at her watch
                        with her atoms
                jiggling
to heaven

Self Explanatory

this man's walking,
                      coming,
with an aura of finality,
            towards me
                    with his hands
                            in his trouser pockets
and a coiled smile on his
                crumbly face
which becomes a huge laugh as he
                      looks into my eyes
            and passes
and keeps on walking,
                        walks
          around the corner
and into *Harvies Bar*
                or the off licence
                      or wherever it is
            people go
when they go around the corner
and leaves me wondering
                what the hell it was
he was laughing at
when he looked into my eyes,
                    perhaps
                    he found something
deep and meaningful there, something
he recognised, something he'd forgotten
and I made him remember,
                perhaps
there's some toothpaste
                  on my chin
or my hair's sticking up
                  like Stan Laurel's,
        perhaps
he's only laughing at the fact that

                        he and I are going to die
and there's nothing we can do about it
            even if we wanted to,
                                    or maybe
        it's just because my fly's down
and everyone knows
except me

Tour de Paisley

a two-wheeled ned
wearing
a red polka dot
King of the Mountains t-shirt
is being nicked
by the filth
outside *BETFRED*

At the Third Stroke

of 11 a.m.
at Paisley Cenotaph

a brown-bomber-jacketed
stubble-scratching
morning-after jakey

is probably wondering
Whit thi fuck ur
aw theez peepul dayn here
ut this time uh thi day?

as he wanders
contentedly
between

the ribboned
and medalled ranks
and the silent lowered flags

Requiem for the Fallen

Seven
blue-sweatered belligerents
with golden threaded epaulettes
on a military night off
from the SAS, or the SBS,
or the Bank of Scotland,
embark
the Glasgow clockwork tube
at two identical doors
equidistant from each other
and stand there
              swaying,
                          laughing,
saying
fuck fuck fuck fuck
to each other,
and doing V-signs,
and *You're a wanker* wanking mimes
to each other,
and stretching their arms out
                          to keep
a balance,
      belching,
saying

Thi rule is yi canni touch
thi fuckin sides   *yi huv*
ti go thi whole way
withoot touchin thi fuckin sides
and
That's a fuckin stupit rule
and doing
You're a wanker wanking mimes
to each other,
the language of love,

as all the survivors on the parallel seats
are thinking to ourselves
        that the world is
   a safer place
in their hands,
and giggling like ancient children
while saying *fuck fuck fuck fuck*
and *This is so fuckin easy*
        until the train
     stops
  and they all fall
down

Wealth of Nations

at the graceful curve
into Sauchiehall Street

the almost-not-there ghost words
ANK OF SCOTLAND
can be seen to the right
of STARBUCKS COFFEE

and immediately below the
CHARING CROSS MANSIONS
ornamental clock
which is currently stopped
at midnight or noon

The Knowledge

a man behind a titanic
back-of-a-shop bin
keeks over the lid
and smiles
and shouts
See you taxi drivers
yir aw fuckin pricks!
with an accent
of intoxication
in the direction
of the taxi drivers ranked up
outside Queen Street Station

the cabbies
can't hear what he's saying,
don't know he's there

unlike the rest of us
who laugh
as we dodge
between the rain drops
to reach our trains
with somewhere to go in our heads
and lacking the wisdom
to tell if he's wrong or right

The Edge

the woman tells the man
that he's just stepped
in the dog's jobby
on the pavement outside
an off licence
as he's pushing the buggy
with the grand-child in it
dreaming, oblivious,
but
he doesn't seem
to understand
as she tells him
he'll have to scrape
his shoe on the edge of the pavement
to take it off
as she points back at the place
where they've just come from,
the time all gone,
where the fat clot of stepped-in jobby
is still lying and saying
There it is   A big dog's jobby
And YOU stood in it

Divided Selfie

two grown-up girls
in grey hoods
      swaying side by side
       on swing-park swings

heads down,
saying nothing

      taking selfies
     of themselves
to send to each other
when it's all been said

Social Comment

an employee in the park
with slender red pincers

is briefly relaxing
his grip on the handle

and releasing
a black empty can

into his
environmentally-conscious

transparently-green Council bag
full of garbage

while creating
a majestic belch

Catholic Pigeon

a ned with
a UNION BEARS
     NO SURRENDER
sticker
stuck
to his JD bag

flicks his fag
at a wee bird's head

George Square Thatcher Death Horse

a Saltire with the words
FUCK THE TORIES written on it
is relentlessly held aloft
at the same time as Tommy Sheridan
is shouting louder than anyone has shouted
in the history of everyone
from the top deck of a discobus
about the Hillsborough 96
and the crushed communities
and milk
greed
mines
steel
and how the dead creature really said
glory in inequality
and called Mandela a *grubby little terrorist*.
and a man wearing a Rangers scarf
is replying *Quack Quack!*
and a figure with a horse's head
like a remnant from a myth
is checking the voices
on its mobile phone
and Wonder Woman is banging
out of time on her red tambourine
as others swiftly cross the space
on their way home from work
with briefcases in their hands
and the future echoing
and eyes looking straight ahead.

Mogwai CDs Covered in Dust

the red chair was carried
and placed on the kitchen floor,
I stood
beside it
then on it without falling
and scanned the long line of CDs above my head
on the shelf skinned with dust
because I haven't been up here in a long time
with my eyes
searching amongst Love
and The Blue Nile and Crosby
Stills Nash and
Bartok,
while hunting in particular
for *Rock Action* by Mogwai
with the photo of them peeping over the edge
of a mysterious pool table in Glasgow. it's been
far too long since I put them on,
the hard bits,
soft bits,
anger, tenderness
which drills deep within
to the inevitable frightening absence of man.

Fine

Three weeks ago
I met a man
I used to work in the same place as
on the cobbles beside the river.

The sun was high.
He said *I'm doing fine*.
I said *I'm doing fine*.

He said he is in
a lower position
somewhere else
but there is no responsibility
and he can sleep at night
in his bed.

It feels good to do it
without dreaming,
without waking up.

We said *Goodbye*.
I knew his name.
The swans slid by
with three cygnets
past the mud-trash PC,
the reflected star.

One day later
I told two men
I used to work in the same place as
that I'd met him on the cobbles
and he said *I'm doing fine*.

We talked in silence,
drank each other's drinks.

Now
I can't remember his name.
I've been travelling inside
the alphabet
trying to make a connection,
the leap.

He was a lawyer.
I don't imagine it matters.
The sun was high.
We're all doing fine.

Nothing is mine.
The mind is white.

**The Story of Human Afflictions
Without Having to Catch Any of Them**

you got your chicken pox
you got your smallpox
you got your mumps

you got your labyrinthitis
you got your gastroenteritis
you got your impetigo

you got your hepatitis A
you got your hepatitis B
you got your rickets

you got your lassa fever
you got your legionnaire's disease
you got your ringworm

you got your tetanus
you got your tinnitus
you got your neurofibromatosis

you got your rabies
you got your scabies
you got your lumbago

you got your pre-menstrual tension
you got your postnatal depression
you got your hot flushes

you got your bubonic plague
you got your pneumonic plague
you got your runny nose

you got your premature ejaculation
you got your erectile dysfunction
you got your itchy balls

you got your whooping cough
you got your diphtheria
you got your thrush

you got your tennis elbow
you got your golfer's elbow
you got your athlete's foot

you got your irritable bowel syndrome
you got your haemorrhoids
you got your anal fistula

you got your Alzheimer's
you got your Parkinson's
you got your cerebral palsy

you got your motor neuron disease
you got your Munchausen's Syndrome
you got your Acquired Immune Deficiency Syndrome

you got your Asian flu
you got your Spanish flu
you got your Swine flu

you got your malaria
you got your cholera
you got your ingrown toenail

you got your deep vein thrombosis
you got your coronary thrombosis
you got your dandruff

you got your shingles
you got your SAD
you got your winter vomiting

you got your ME
you got your TB
you got your BIG C

you got your agonising death
you got your slow death
you got your quick death

you got your death rattle
you got your rigor mortis
you got your decomposition

you got your sorry-if-I-missed-out-
your-favourite-but-there's-only-so-
much-time
you got your it's-a-frickin-miracle-that-
we-got-this-far-at-all
you got your spending-the-rest-of-your-life-
wondering-what-you're-going-to-get-and-
when-you're-going-to-get-it-or-if-you-
already-have-it

you got your floating-towards-the-ceiling
you got your going-towards-the-light-at-
the-end-of-the-tunnel
you got your choice

you got your heaven

you got your hell

you got your

Club Arthritis

Welcome to Club Arthritis
where your knees
begin to ache,
and your elbows begin
to ache,
and your shoulders begin to
ache,
and the bits between your elbows
and shoulders
begin to ache.
and your hips begin to ache,
and your back begins to ache,
and your aches begin to ache,
and you look at yourself
in the mirror in the morning
and know that everything has changed
but you can't put your finger
on it.

something further
than your own eyes.

and your fingers look strange,
and life begins to ache,
and you can't remember
what you went into a room for,
and you can't remember
what you came out of a room for.
and it's becoming clear
that nature is saying
You've done your bit to contribute
to the procreation of the species
which is exactly hee-haw
and you're now surplus to requirements
so it's time you were gone as fast

as you can. Off you pop.

and you can't remember
what you went into a room for,
and you can't remember
what you came out of a room for.
and you can't remember
if you're writing the same thing
you wrote two minutes before.
and your eyes disintegrate,
and your story
disintegrates,
and then you get cancer and die.

Welcome to Pointless

sitting on my seat watching *Pointless*
with Alexander Armstrong
and it slowly
seeps
through
that I've heard this question before
and the eccentric contestants
from every corner of the British Isles
look horribly familiar
and I'm sure I've already heard
one of them say
that he collects paper clips.
and it dawns
that this is a repeat
and I've heard everything before
I'm redoing part of existence that
I've already done.
and the audience are laughing
in the same places,
and I still know the answers
I knew first time round
such as who sang *Maggie May*
and who sang *Carrie-Anne*
and I still don't know the answers
I didn't know first time round
such as who's the black and white
foreign minister in the bottom left hand corner
and the nationalities of Formula 1 drivers
such as Emerson Fittipaldi.
I search
in the weekend newspaper TV supplement
to see if there's an R for Repeat next to *Pointless*
for this exact second in my life
because if there is then it's my own mistake
but if there isn't then I'll feel cheated

and soiled
and it's something
I'll never be able to forgive.

Withdrawal Symptom

a girl with
the crack of

her arse
on display

pulls up
her pants

as she runs
to the bank

The Bank

down to the bank to dump my bulging bag
of empties
into the family-size purple bin
already brimming
at this time on a Sunday
with colourful glass
covered
in colourful labels
for necessities such as
Budweiser   jalapeno pickle
marmite   medium dry champagne
green bottle gin   Tesco's own brand gin
invisible vodka   Scotch whisky
red wine   white wine
red rum   white rum
Crabbie's alcoholic ginger beer
for alcoholics
as I covertly push them through
the brush-edged orifice
and lower them as far as I can
into the dark
before letting go
like a parent releasing his child
and listening to them
CRASH
against
the ones already there
as quietly as possible
in case I suddenly feel a hand
on my shoulder and look round
and it's one of my neighbourhood watch neighbours
who says *Is that
last night's empties you're dumping Graham?*
before laughing denouncingly
like this

Hahahahahahahahahahahahahaha
to alert the whole town
who'll bound
in their paisley pattern witch-hunt dressing gowns
to see what it is I'm dumping this week
on top of the same ones I dumped last week

Large Hardon Collider

they   whoever
they are
think they've
found something found how everything
works found something that travels
faster than faster than the speed of light it's
neutrinos or particles
or quarks or particles or something
like that the large hadron collider or
something like that the
large higgs boson hardon collider faster than
the speed of light which everyone thinks
it's not possible
to go faster than the speed
of light they said but maybe it is but maybe it
is for god's sake do you see
SEE
exactly   what
exactly
what
this means to everyone here whoever
we are alive in the world today we could
ping to the end of the universe
and piss on our territory
erect a flag,
or travel back, or travel back in
time to
reconstruct things that have already
happened
to suit the future us whoever that
is wherever that is I suppose but maybe we've already
been doing it for years, already
been altering us for years   years   maybe
they   whoever
they are

have been doing it for years   whoever
we are, we thought
we've found
something that thinks faster than   faster
faster than faster than the speed of dark

Suddenly I Remember The Dog and The Man

n the winter dark
a terrier wagging dog
thesmudge of white
a colour
off the lwash
off the leash
is too full
of
is too eagir
far too eager
to try to leap on the
correct change required
double decker bus
tpo go somehwere
to go somewhere
so nce
so fast
which is
drawqing up
drawing nup
drawing up
to the stop
at the foot of the hill
and runs too sun
and runs too soon
and slips
and slipsquickly
under the big front
left wheelk
is dead
n the slice of an eye,
an old man
who owms it
who owns
it

even out of life
doesn't want to say anything,
doesn't need an expression
as if he knew all thew time
it as going
it was going
to happen exactlylike this
all along somedaytoday,
lifts and turns
it al white
and soft
an dead
and dead
in his old tender old arms
and looks at it
in his arms
back beyond the hill
nd the bus
petrols away

Complete Dummy

a truck
                      is stuck at the lights
          with the driver holding the wheel
and watching straight ahead
                        and a dummy with a female wig
          in the passenger seat beside him

           she's wearing
    a belt
which means he must
                  be concerned for her welfare
and doesn't want her to smash head first into the windscreen
          when he slams on his brakes
to avoid the child

              or the pensioner,
      or the dog

he probably just wants
someone to talk to on dark nights
                    about Albert Camus
or the melting of the polar ice caps
                      or a cure for cancer,
         which they'll certainly
find in the future
when he's long dead

                    everyone
      needs a point in their life,
                  everyone
needs a constant, a comfort,
              like the distance of the sun,
        and the face
on the moon

Tenements of Mars

Every pane on
a Paisley back street
reflecting the H.G.Wells-red
of the sunrise.

Humanless pavement.
Dog turds, waiting.

End of the World,
followed by rain.

Micro Biology

1.
in the park,
at the edge of
the rain

a running woman,
pushing
her pram

a man on a bench,
head in
his hand

2.
Mummy

do you know
do you know
do you know

do you know
what a worm turns into?

No sweetheart,
what does a worm
turn into?

It turns
it turns
it turns

it turns into   A caterpillar!

And what do you
turn into
sweetheart?

I don't
i don't
i don't

i don't turn into   Anything

Printed in the USA
CPSIA information can be obtained
at www.ICGtesting.com
LVHW040948101124
796216LV00004B/39